Ever

of 1934

News for every day of the year

New Zealand aviatrix Jean Batten breaks the
speed record for a solo female flight from
England to Australia, 30 May 1934.

By Hugh Morrison

MONTPELIER PUBLISHING

Front cover (clockwise from left): The England to Australia Air Race begins on 20 October. Luggage ticket for the RMS *Queen Mary*, launched on 26 September. Claudette Colbert stars in the title role in *Cleopatra*, released on 16 August. Ginger Rogers stars in *The Gay Divorcee*, released on 12 October. Work begins on the prototoype Vokswagen car on 22 June.

Back cover (clockwise from top): Wallace Beery and Jackie Cooper in *Treasure Island,* released on 17 August. The cartoon strip 'L'il Abner' is first published on 13 August. The gangsters Bonnie and Clyde are shot dead on 23 May. Shirley Temple's first film is released on 19 April. Johnny Weismuller stars in *Tarzan and his Mate*, released on 20 April. The Flying Scotsman breaks the world rail speed record on 30 November.

Image credits: George E Marsh, Jack de Nijs, Roger Pick, Legend Photography.

Published in Great Britain by Montpelier Publishing.
Printed and distributed by Amazon KDP.
This edition © 2023. All rights reserved.

ISBN: 9798856842189

January
1934

Monday 1: Liberty, the National Council for Civil Liberties, is founded in the UK.

Tuesday 2: One of the earliest works of narrative relief sculpture, the Warka Vase (dating from around 3000 BC) is found in Iraq.

Wednesday 3: US President Franklin D Roosevelt gives his State of the Union address, the first time it has been done so in January.

Flash Gordon makes his first appearance on 7 January.

Thursday 4: The Henschel HS121 aeroplane is first flown.

Friday 5: The record producer and sound engineer Phil Ramone is born in South Africa (died 2013).

Saturday 6: The pro-Nazi German State Church introduces sweeping powers to dismiss officials who oppose the government, leading to the resignation of hundreds of clergymen.

Sunday 7: Flash Gordon first appears in a newspaper comic strip in the USA.

January 1934

The Curtiss XF13C-1 monoplane makes its first flight.

Monday 8: The champion French cyclist Jacques Anquetil is born in Mont-Saint-Aignan, France (died 1987).

Tuesday 9: Paul Manship's statue *Prometheus* is unveiled at the Rockefeller Center in New York City.

Wednesday 10: Princess Elizabeth of Greece and Denmark marries Count Carl Thedor in Bavaria.

Richard Briers is born on 14 January.

Thursday 11: A convoy of US Navy flying boats travel from San Francisco to Hawaii in a record 24 hours 35 minutes.

Friday 12: Indian nationalist leader Surya Sen is executed for his role in the Chittagong Uprising of 1930 in which 80 Indian Army soldiers were killed.

Saturday 13: The scientist Paul Ulrich Villard, discoverer of gamma-rays, dies aged 73.

The Curtiss XF13C-1 monoplane first flies on 7 January.

Sunday 14: The De Havilland Express passenger aeroplane flies for the first time.

Actor Richard Briers (*The Good Life*) is born in Raynes Park, Surrey (died 2013).

Monday 15: At least 6000 people are killed when an earthquake hits Bihar, India.

Above: the Jonker Diamond is found on 17 January.

Above: Tom Baker is born on 20 January.

Ramon Grau is forced to resign as President of Cuba and is replaced by Carlos Hevia.

Tuesday 16: A prison guard is killed when notorious gangster Clyde Darrow stages a breakout of five prisoners from Eastham Unit jail, Texas.

Wednesday 17: Carlos Hevia resigns as President of Cuba after only three days in office.

One of the largest diamonds ever discovered, the Jonker Diamond, is found at Elandsfontein Mine in South Africa.

Thursday 18: Manuel Marquez Sterling takes over as President of Cuba, only to be replaced by Carlos Mendiata on the same day; who becomes the island's fourth president in just three days.

Friday 19: The Belgian composer Armande Parent dies aged 71.

Saturday 20: The Japanese photographic company Fuji is established.

The actor Tom Baker (*Dr Who*) is born in Liverpool, England.

Sunday 21: A British Union of Fascists rally in Birmingham, led by Oswald Mosley, attracts a crowd of 10,000.

London is hit by a 'pea souper' fog so thick that it disrupts a performance at the Royal Albert Hall by singer Amelita Galli-Curci.

Monday 22: The German Catholic theologian Karl Adam denounces the Nazis.

January 1934

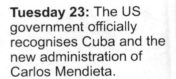

The notorious gangster John Dillinger is arrested on 25 January.

Tuesday 23: The US government officially recognises Cuba and the new administration of Carlos Mendieta.

Wednesday 24: The *Tarzan* actor Johnny Weissmuller separates from actress wife Lupe Velez after being married for just three months.

Thursday 25: The notorious gangster John Dillinger and his 'moll', Billie Frechette, are arrested in Tucson, Arizona.

Friday 26: A ten-year non-aggression pact between Poland and Germany is signed in Berlin.

A failed kidnap and extortion attempt is made on actress Mary Pickford at the Ritz-Carlton Hotel in Boston, Mass.

Above: Mary Pickford, who escapes a kidnap attempt on 26 January.

Saturday 27: An unsuccessful assassination attempt is made on Harmodio Arias Madrid, President of Panama.

Camille Chautemps, Prime Minister of France, resigns following a financial scandal.

Sunday 28: Edouard Deladier is appointed Prime Minister of France following Camille Chautemps' resignation.

The US First Lady, Eleanor Roosevelt, announces that when Prohibition ends in Washington, DC, in February, American wines will be served at formal dinners but no spirits will be permitted.

Monday 29: HM Queen Mary is obliged to 'hitch hike' en route from Sandringham to Cambridge when the royal car breaks down. A passing commercial traveller, a Mr Percy Tidmouth, gives the Queen a lift in his car.

The German chemist and Nobel prize laureate, Fritz Haber, dies aged 65.

Tuesday 30: Three Soviet pilots are killed when their high-altitude balloon *Osoaviakhim-1* crashes following a record ascent to 13.6 miles (22km).

Artist Salvador Dali marries Elena Diakonova.

Wednesday 31: The bank robber Verne Sankey, one of the most wanted men in the USA, is captured in Chicago.

Georgy Bibikov's painting of the doomed Soviet balloonists on 30 January.

February 1934

Thursday 1: Greece defaults on its promise to deport the US fugitive Samuel Insull, wanted on charges of bank fraud.

Friday 2: Germany bans monarchist organisations.

Saturday 3: The notorious gangster Aussie Elliott is killed in a shoot-out with police near Sapulpa, Oklahoma.

Sunday 4: Cuba launches a new constitution.

Monday 5: Surrealist artists in Paris hold a mock-trial of Salvador Dali; many of them are communists and take umbrage with some of his right-wing views.

Tuesday 6: 17 people are shot dead by police in Paris after left and right wing groups clash in the Place de la Concorde.

Wednesday 7: France's Prime Minister Edouard Deladier resigns over the killing of demonstrators by police in Paris on 6 February.

Thursday 8: Britain's Cunard and White Star shipping lines merge.

The 'trial' of Salvador Dali is held on 5 February.

Friday 9: Greece, Turkey, Romania and Yugoslavia sign the Balkan Pact.

Gaston Doumergue becomes Prime Minister of France.

Saturday 10: The poet Fleur Adcock is born in Auckland, New Zealand.

The King and Queen of Siam (now Thailand) arrive in France as part of a seven month world tour.

Sunday 11: Fashion designer Mary Quant is born in Blackheath, London.

Monday 12: A four-day civil war breaks out in Austria.

King Prajadhipok of Siam begins his world tour on 10 February.

Tuesday 13: 104 people abandon the sinking Soviet steamship SS *Chelyuskin* in the Arctic and manage to find safety on an iceberg; they are not rescued until two months later.

Actor George Segal is born on Long Island, New York.

Wednesday 14: Germany abolishes the Reichsrat, the parliamentary upper chamber.

Left: The SS *Chelyuskin* is abandoned on 13 February.

February 1934

Above: Nicaraguan rebel leader Augusto Sandino is assassinated on 21 February.

Barry Humphries is born on 17 February.

The swindler Charles Ponzi, after whom the Ponzi Scheme (pyramid scheme) is named, is released after 11 years of imprisonment in the USA.

Thursday 15: The Social Democrat Party of Austria is banned.

Friday 16: The Noel Coward musical *Conversation Piece* opens in London.

The Austrian Civil War ends.

Saturday 17: The King of Belgium is killed in a climbing accident aged 58.

The actor Barry Humphries (Dame Edna Everage) is born in Melbourne, Australia (died 2023).

The actor Alan Bates is born in Allestree, Derbyshire.

Sunday 18: The Spanish fashion designer Paco Rabanne is born in Pasaia, Spain. (died 2023).

Monday 19: The body of King Albert of Belgium is brought to Brussels to lie in state.

Tuesday 20: The British MP and future Prime Minister Anthony Eden meets Adolf Hitler in Berlin to encourage Germany to continue with disarmament.

Wednesday 21: The Nicaraguan rebel leader Augusto Sandino is assassinated.

Thursday 22: *It Happened One Night,* starring Clark Gable and Claudette Colbert is released. It is notable for being the first feature film to show a woman wearing pyjamas and for showing an unmarried couple sharing a hotel room.

Clark Gable and Claudette Colbert star in *It Happened One Night*, released on 22 February.

Sir Edward Elgar dies on 23 February.

Friday 23: Leopold III is crowned King of the Belgians.

The composer Sir Edward Elgar dies aged 76.

Saturday 24: Adolf Hitler leads celebrations in Germany for the fourteenth anniversary of the National Socialist Programme, the political manifesto which spawned the Nazi Party.

Sunday 25: The actor Bernard Bresslaw, famous for the *Carry On* comedies, is born in London (died 1993).

Monday 26: Ralph Capone, brother of gangster Al Capone, is released from jail following a four year sentence for tax evasion.

Tuesday 27: The three Bulgarians accused of burning down Germany's Reichstag (parliament) in 1933 are deported to the USSR.

Wednesday 28: British hunger marchers are met at the House of Commons by Labour MPs.

March 1934

Thursday 1: Puyi, the last Emperor of China, is enthroned in the Japanese puppet state of Manchukuo.

The spiritualist writer Charles Webster Leadbetter dies aged 60.

Primo Carnera beats Tommy Loughran to gain the world heavyweight boxing title in Madison Square Garden, New York City.

Friday 2: (Good Friday) The world's first high-speed streamlined train service, the M-10000, goes into service between Kansas City, Missouri, and Salina, Kansas.

Primo Carnera becomes world heavyweight boxing champ on 1 March.

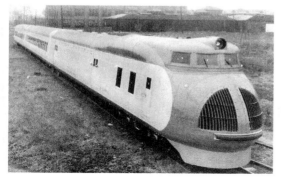

The world's first high speed streamlined diesel train goes into operation on 2 March. It includes aeroplane style seat-tray dining.

Saturday 3: The notorious gangster John Dillinger escapes from Crown Point Jail, Indiana.

Sunday 4: (Easter Sunday). The Mount Davidson Cross in San Francisco, commemorating the dead of the 1915 Armenian genocide, is dedicated.

Monday 5: The German government bans all Jewish actors from appearing on stage.

A severe earthquake hits Wellington, New Zealand; fortunately only two people are killed.

Yuri Gagarin is born on 9 March.

Tuesday 6: Gangster John Dillinger and his gang rob a bank of $49,000 in Sioux Falls, South Dakota.

Wednesday 7: The notorious gangster 'West Side' Frankie Pope is killed in a shootout with police in Chicago, Illinois.

Thursday 8: The British government announces four new squadrons for the Royal Air Force, stating that Britain's aim is to have 'parity in the air' with the world's major powers.

March 1934

Friday 9: Yuri Gagarin, the first man in space, is born in Klushino, USSR (died 1968).

Saturday 10: The US government announces the end of all restrictions on the importation of foreign alcohol, following the end of Prohibition in 1933.

Sunday 11: The Austrian government authorises the sacking of any private employee who takes part in anti-government demonstrations.

Monday 12: The Estonian leader Konstantin Pats shuts down all political opposition and declares martial law in order to crush the emerging populist Vaps Movement.

Germany bans Jews from joining the armed forces.

Tuesday 13: Gangster John Dillinger raids the First National Bank in Mason City, Iowa, escaping with $52,000.

Wednesday 14: The historical film *The House of Rothschild* starring Boris Karloff is released.

Adolf Hitler refuses to accept a French disarmament proposal for Germany.

Thursday 15: US legal adviser Allen Dulles issues a seven-point plan for European disarmament to prevent a second world war.

Frank Lawton and Ursual Jeans star in *Cavalcade*, which wins an Academy Award on 16 March.

Horton Smith wins the first US Masters on 22 March.

Friday 16: *Cavalcade* wins Best Picture in the 6th Academy Awards (Oscars.

Saturday 17: Austria, Hungary and Italy sign the Rome Protocols for mutual economic support.

Cambridge wins the 86th Boat Race.

Sunday 18: Benito Mussolini announces a 60-year plan for Italian colonisation of Africa.

Monday 19: Pope Pius XI canonises three new saints: Giuseppe Benedetto Cottolengo, Pompilio Maria Pirrotti and Teresa Margaret of the Sacred Heart.

Tuesday 20: The Dowager Queen Emma of the Netherlands dies aged 75.

Wednesday 21: 2000 people die in the Great Hakodate Fire which destroys much of the city of Hakodate, Japan.

Thursday 22: The first US Masters golf tournament is won by Horton Smith.

Friday 23: Golden Miller wins the Grand National.

Saturday 24: US President Franklin Roosevelt signs the Phillippines Independence Act promising self rule for the colony by 1944.

Sunday 25: A general election takes place in Italy to rubber-stamp Mussolini's hold on power; it is the last election to be held in the country until 1948.

Mussolini is re-elected on 25 March.

March 1934

Monday 26: Germany announces the Strength Through Joy programme of free holiday cruises for workers.

Tuesday 27: A bill to make Hawaii a state of the USA is announced. The territory does not become part of the USA until 1959.

Wednesday 28: Chancellor Dollfuss, leader of Austria, bans the media from making jokes about his small stature of just 4 feet 11 inches (1.52m).

Richard Chamberlain is born on 31 March.

Thursday 29: Germany bans the new boxing film *The Prizefighter and the Lady* because its star, Max Baer, is Jewish.

Friday 30: Zeppo Marx leaves the Marx Brothers comedy troupe.

Saturday 31: Germany's oldest newspaper, *Vossiche Zeitung*, first published in 1704, voluntarily closes down in the light of a Nazi clampdown on the freedom of the press.

The actor Richard Chamberlain (*Dr Kildare*) is born in Beverly Hills, California.

April 1934

Sunday 1: Two police officers are killed in a shootout with the infamous 'Bonnie and Clyde' gang in Grapevine, Texas.

The 19th century Italian priest Don Bosco is canonised by Pope Pius XI.

Monday 2: Guy Moll wins the Monaco Grand Prix motor race.

The Roman Catholic Holy Year of 1933 (commemorating 1900 years since Christ's death and resurrection) officially ends.

Tuesday 3: German courts ban Roman Catholic newspapers and magazines.

Myrna Loy and Elizabeth Allen star in the controversial medical drama, *Men in White*, released on 6 April.

April 1934

Leon Trotsky is found hiding in France on 15 April.

Wednesday 4: The Soviet-Polish Non-Aggression Pact of 1932 is renewed for a further ten years.

Thursday 5: Joan Meakin becomes the first female glider pilot to fly over the English Channel.

Friday 6: The film *Men in White* starring Clark Gable and Myrna Loy is released.

Saturday 7: At least 50 people die when a landslide causes a tsunami in a fjord near Tajford, Norway.

Sunday 8: Left and right-wing groups clash in street fighting in Paris.

Monday 9: Pope Pius XI invites 80 journalists to the first ever press conference to be held in the Vatican.

Tuesday 10: A failed assassination attempt is made on the Spanish fascist leader Jose Antonio Primo de Rivera.

Jean Cocteau's play *The Infernal Machine* opens in Paris.

Wednesday 11: Italian pilot Renato Donati sets a new flight altitude record of 47,354 feet (14,433 m).

Thursday 12: Costa Rica, El Salvador, Guatemala, Honduras and Nicaragua sign a treaty of friendship.

Friday 13: The renegade American financier Samuel Insull, wanted on fraud charges, is handed over to US authorities in Smyrna, Turkey.

Saturday 14: The actress Norma Talmadge is divorced from Joseph Schenck.

Sunday 15: Exiled Soviet politician Leon Trotsky is found hiding in France, after having fled his previous residence in Corsica over

The first film starring Shirley Temple is released on 19 April.

fears of attempts on his life. He is eventually assassinated in 1940.

Monday 16: The title 'Hero of the Soviet Union' is established as the highest award in the Soviet honours system.

Tuesday 17: Britain's Chancellor of the Exchequer Neville Chamberlain presents a 'prosperity budget' with tax cuts and a projected surplus of £800,000.

Wednesday 18: The world's first launderette (laundromat) opens in Fort Worth, Texas.

Thursday 19: The film *Stand Up And Cheer* is released, starring Shirley Temple in her first major role.

Friday 20: The film *Tarzan and His Mate*, the second Tarzan film to star Johnny Weissmuller, is released.

Germany's Gestapo (secret police) is taken over by Heinrich Himmler.

Saturday 21: The *Daily Mail* publishes what is claimed to be the first photograph of the Loch Ness Monster, taken by a London

Left: the world's first self-service laundrette, called a 'washateria', opens in Fort Worth, Texas on 18 April.

April 1934

Tarzan and his Mate **is released on 20 April.**

surgeon, Robert Kenneth Wilson. In 1975 the photograph is revealed as a hoax.

Sunday 22: The Appenine Base Tunnel in Italy, the world's longest double-track train tunnel to this date, is opened by King Victor Emmanuel III.

Monday 23: The actress Gloria Swanson announces her divorce from husband F Michael Farmer.

Actress Norma Talmadge marries George Jessel.

Tuesday 24: The Hammond Organ is patented.

The actress Shirley MacLaine is born in Richmond, Virginia.

Wednesday 25: A six year old heiress, June Robles, is kidnapped in Tucson, Arizona, and a $15,000 ransom demanded for her return. This sparks one of the largest manhunts in US history. On 14 May she is eventually found alive and well, locked in a metal box in the Arizona desert. Her abductors are never caught.

The first photograph purporting to be of the Loch Ness Monster is published on 21 April; it is later revealed as a hoax.

Shirley MacLaine (shown here in 1960) is born on 24 April.

Englebert Dollfuss takes over Austria on 30 April.

Thursday 26: University of Nevada scientists Paul Hartman and Angelo Granata successfully transmit recorded music via a beam of light. The technological breakthrough allows the eventual development of the compact disc in the 1980s.

Friday 27: Wanda T Stewart, described by police as 'the second most dangerous criminal in the USA' (after gangster John Dillinger), is shot dead after escaping from San Quentin prison.

Saturday 28: Manchester City defeats Portsmouth 2-1 in the FA Cup Final at Wembley Stadium, London.

Sunday 29: The 9th Panchen Lama, second in command of the secretive nation of Tibet, returns from exile in China following the death of the 13th Dalai Lama.

Monday 30: The Austrian parliament votes to dissolve itself, turning the country into a dictatorship under Englebert Dollfuss.

May
1934

The Three Stooges make their first screen appearance on 5 May.

Tuesday 1: Austria's new constitution is proclaimed, with the country's name changed from 'Republic' to 'Federal State'.

Wednesday 2: Actress Virginia Bruce files for divorce from the Hollywood actor John Gilbert.

Two Germans, a Frenchman and a Pole are arrested in Paris following the discovery of a plot to transmit French military secrets to Germany in coded messages disguised to look like love letters.

Thursday 3: The boxer Sir Henry Cooper is born in Oxted, Surrey (died 2011).

Singer Frankie Valli is born in Newark, New Jersey.

Friday 4: The crime drama film *Manhattan Melodrama* starring Clark Gable and Myrna Loy is released.

Major fires destroy large tracts of forest in the Blue Ridge Mountains, North Carolina.

Sir Henry Cooper is born on 3 May.

Saturday 5: Cavalcade wins the Kentucky Derby.

The first Three Stooges comedy film, *Women Haters*, is released.

Sunday 6: Large crowds led by the high ranking Nazi Joseph Goebbels stage a protest against the occupation of the former German province of Saarland, under the control of British and French authorities since the end of the First World War.

Monday 7: Following a series of fatal crashes, the US Army loses the contract to deliver airmail, and the service is taken over by a civilian contractor.

Tuesday 8: The fugitive financier Samuel Insoll, wanted on fraud charges, is returned to the USA after being arrested in Turkey and put on remand to face trial. He is later acquitted.

Wednesday 9: The worst 'dust bowl' storm of the Great Depression takes place in the midwestern USA.

An 83-day strike of all waterfront workers on the US western seaboard begins.

The playwright Alan Bennett is born in Leeds, Yorkshire.

Left: a 'dust bowl' storm. The worst occurrence of this in the 1930s takes place on 9 May in the US midwest.

May 1934

**Alan Bennett
is born on 9 May.**

Thursday 10: Germany's foreign minister Joachim Von Ribbentrop holds talks with Britain's foreign secretary Sir John Simon over the contentious issue of German rearmament, strictly controlled since the end of the First World War.

Friday 11: The Gestapo breaks up a meeting of 1000 anti-Nazi church leaders in Brandenburg, Germany.

Saturday 12: *Cocktails for Two* by Duke Ellington and his Orchestra hits number one in the US charts.

Sunday 13: An armistice is signed in the Saudi-Yemeni War.

High Quest wins the Preakness Stakes horse race.

Monday 14: The six-year old heiress June Robles, kidnapped on 25 April, is found alive and well by police in the Arizona desert after a nationwide search; her abductors are never identified.

Tuesday 15: Karis Ulmanis takes power in Latvia following a military coup.

Wednesday 16: 7000 merchant seamen join the ongoing large-scale waterfront strike on the USA's west coast.

The Black Cat is released on 18 May.

Thursday 17: The American pro-Nazi group Friends of New Germany holds a rally in New York City attended by 20,000 supporters.

Friday 18: The horror film *The Black Cat* starring Boris Karloff and Bela Lugosi is released.

Saturday 19: General Kimon Georgiev seizes control of Bulgaria in a military coup.

Sunday 20: Germany's St Conrad of Parzham is canonised by Pope Pius XI, who uses the opportunity to criticise the country's falling away from Catholic values into National Socialism.

Gustav Holst dies on 25 May.

Monday 21: A major fire in the Chicago Stockyards district causes damage costing over US$10 million.

Tuesday 22: US President Roosevelt calls on a ban of arms sales to Bolivia and Paraguay to prevent the escalation of war between the two countries.

Wednesday 23: The notorious outlaws Bonnie and Clyde are killed in a carefully planned police ambush near Sailes, Louisiana.

The crime thriller *The Thin Man* starring William Powell and Myrna Loy is released.

Bonnie and Clyde are killed when their car is riddled with bullets on 23 May.

May 1934

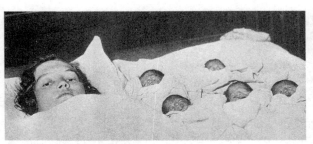

Mrs Elzire Dionne, 25, gives birth to quintuplets on 28 May.

Thursday 24: A strike at the Auto-Lite factory in Toledo, Ohio, turns violent as 6000 workers clash with National Guard troops.

Friday 25: The composer Gustav Holst dies aged 59.

Saturday 26: 'Soft serve' ice-cream (the type served in vans, such as 'Mr Whippy') is born when the van of Tom Carvel, an ice-cream vendor in Hartsdale, New York, suffers a breakdown. Carvel is forced to sell his melting ice-cream, but it proves more popular than when it was hard-frozen.

Sunday 27: An assassination attempt is made on Jefferson Caffery, US Ambassador to Cuba.

Monday 28: The Dionne Quintuplets, the first quintuplets to survive infancy, are born in Corbeil, Ontario.

Tuesday 29: The actress Nanette Newman is born in Norhampton, England.

Wednesday 30: Bill Cummings wins the Indianapolis 500 motor race.

Thursday 31: German Christians sign the Barmen Declaration, marking the beginning of the Confessing Church, the sect opposed to the 'official' pro-Nazi German state church.

June 1934

Pat Boone (shown here in 1960) is born on 1 June.

Friday 1: The comedy film *Little Miss Marker* starring Shirley Temple is released.

The singer Pat Boone is born in Jacksonville, Florida.

Saturday 2: 39 countries sign the London Act, a major international treaty on copyrights, patents and trademarks.

Sunday 3: The Dayton Speedway opens in Ohio.

Monday 4: Britain announces that due to the Great Depression it is unable to maintain its repayment of war debts to the USA.

Tuesday 5: A hurricane hits British Honduras (now Belize) and spreads over central America, resulting in an eventual deathtoll of up to 3000 people.

Wednesday 6: An attempted military coup takes place in Lithuania by supporters of exiled former Prime Minister Augustinus Voldemaras.

The future King Albert II of Belgium is born in Brussels, Belgium.

June 1934

Hitler and Mussolini meet for the first time, on 14 June.

Thursday 7: French cinema owners protest in Paris against proposed restrictions on the importation of American films.

Friday 8: Left-wing protesters disrupt a rally held by British Union of Fascists leader at Olympia, London; the event is called off after two hours.

The Cincinatti Reds become the first US baseball team to travel to a game by air.

Saturday 9: Donald Duck makes his screen debut in the cartoon *The Wise Little Hen.*

Sunday 10: Italy defeats Czechoslovakia 2-1 in the FIFA World Cup finnal in Rome.

The English composer Frederick Delius dies aged 72.

Monday 11: The Geneva Disarmament Conference ends without success.

The newspaper cartoon strip Mandrake the Magician is first published.

Frederick Delius dies on 10 June.

Tuesday 12: All political parties are abolished in Bulgaria following the coup of 19 May.

Wednesday 13: Large protests take place as senior German Nazi official Joseph Goebbels gives a lecture at the University of Warsaw, Poland.

Thursday 14: Adolf Hitler and Benito Mussolini meet for the first time, in Venice, Italy.

Max Baer wins the World Heavyweight Boxing title in Madison Square Garden, New York City.

Max Baer becomes World Heavyweight Boxing champ on 14 June.

Friday 15: A failed assassination attempt takes place on Carlos Mendieta, President of Cuba.

Saturday 16: One person is killed and several million dollars of damage caused when a hurricane hits Baton Rouge, Louisiana.

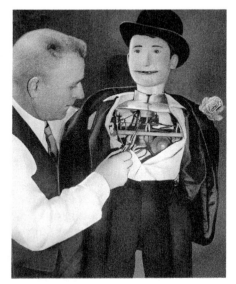

'Willie the Robot' goes berserk at the World's Fair in Chicago on 19 June.

Sunday 17: Germany's Vice-Chancellor Franz von Papen gives the Marburg Speech, the last political address which is openly critical of the Nazis before a clampdown on all dissent.

Monday 18: The Indian Reorganisation Act is passed in the USA, ending previous attempts to assimilate American Indians and instead providing them with specific civil rights and legal freedoms.

Tuesday 19: 'Willie' an experimental robot on display at the World's Fair in Chicago goes berserk during

June 1934

Of Human Bondage is released in cinemas on 28 June.

a performance; it is later found that the erratic behaviour was caused by a small boy in the audience shining a torch into the robot's photoelectric cell, causing it to go haywire.

Wednesday 20: Three people are killed when the German liner SS *Dresden* hits rocks in a Norwegian fjord.

Thursday 21: Turkey makes the use of hereditary surnames compulsory; Turks until this date generally did not use them.

Friday 22: South Africa becomes a sovereign independent state within the British Empire, adopting the Statute of Westminster which also granted autonomy to Canada, Australia and New Zealand.

Auto manufacturer Ferdinand Porsche agrees to design a new vehicle, the Volkswagen ('people's car') for the German government.

Saturday 23: A failed mutiny attempt takes place in the Cuban navy.

Sunday 24: Jimmy Wedell, aircraft designer and test pilot, is killed in a flying accident aged 34.

On 22 June, Ferdinand Porsche (left) begins work on the Volkswagen prototype (above) which is produced later in the year.

Henry Cotton wins the Open on 29 June.

Monday 25: An original manuscript, dating from 1470, of Sir Thomas Malory's *Morte D'Arthur*, the seminal book on the Arthurian legend, is found hidden in the library of Winchester College.

Tuesday 26: France introduces an import tariff on American films so expensive that it amounts to a ban.

Wednesday 27: Britain rejects a US offer to accept goods in lieu of payment of war debt.

Thursday 28: The drama film *Of Human Bondage* starring Bette Davis is released.

Friday 29: Henry Cotton wins the Open golf championships at Sandwich, Kent.

Saturday 30: The 'night of the long knives' takes place as Hitler orders the assassination of 100 of his political opponents.

July
1934

Sunday 1: US President Franklin D Roosevelt begins a tour of American possessions in the Atlantic and Pacific.

Monday 2: Germany's President, Paul von Hindenburg, sends a message congratulating Adolf Hitler on the recent purge of his opponents, claiming it 'rescued the German people from great danger.'

Tuesday 3: The Bank of Canada is founded.

Wednesday 4: The research scientist Marie Curie dies aged 66.

Thursday 5: President Roosevelt becomes the first US President to visit the American possession of Haiti.

Fred Perry (above right) and Jack Crawford, shown here with an umpire. Perry beats Crawford at Wimbledon on 6 July.

Marty Feldman is born on 8 July.

Friday 6: Fred Perry defeats Australia's Jack Crawford in the Men's tennis final at Wimbledon; he is the first Englishman to win in 25 years.

Saturday 7: Dorothy Round Little (UK) defeats Helen Hull Jacobs in the ladies' tennis final at Wimbledon.

Sunday 8: The comedian Marty Feldman is born in London (died 1982).

Monday 9: Heinrich Himmler is placed in command of Germany's new concentration camp programme.

Tuesday 10: Franklin Roosevelt becomes the first sitting US President to visit South America when he arrives in Colombia.

Wednesday 11: After pressure from the government Hollywood introduces the Hays Code for motion pictures, bringing in stricter moral values in storylines. *The World Moves On*, released the following day, is the first film approved by the Code.

The fashion designer Georgio Armani is born in Piacenza, Italy.

Thursday 12: Belgium bans the wearing of political uniforms.

Friday 13: Baseball star Babe Ruth his the 700th home run of his career at Navin Field, Detroit.

The comedy film *The Old Fashioned Way* starring WC Fields is released.

Saturday 14: Comedy star Buster Keaton is declared bankrupt.

Madeleine Carroll stars in *The World Moves On*, **released on 12 July.**

July 1934

Sunday 15: Hans Stuck wins the German Grand Prix.

Monday 16: A general strike begins in San Francisco over conditions for dock workers.

Tuesday 17: Tony Mancini, a nightclub doorman of Brighton, Sussex, is arrested on suspicion of killing two women whose bodies were found in trunks in the city. The case, known as the Brighton Trunk Murders, causes a press sensation. The two killings are later found to be unconnected; no killer is found for the first but Mancini is tried and acquitted for the second. In a strange twist, in 1976 he admits he *did* commit the second murder.

Wednesday 18: Liverpool's Queensway Tunnel is opened by HM King George V; it is the longest underwater tunnel to this date.

Thursday 19: San Francisco's general strike ends.

Friday 20: A general strike breaks out in Minneapolis, Minnesota; 68 people are injured in clashes between strikers and police.

Saturday 21: 200,000 are left homeless when the River Vistula bursts its banks in Warsaw, Poland.

The writer and comedian Dr Jonathan Miller (*Beyond the Fringe*) is born in London (died 2019).

Rene Dreyfus wins the Belgian Grand Prix on 29 July in an Alfa-Romeo P3.

John Wayne stars in *The Star Packer*, released on 30 July.

Sunday 22: The notorious gangster John Dillinger, on the run from jail, is shot dead by police in Chicago.

Monday 23: Eight alleged Japanese spies are executed in the USSR for sabotage attacks.

Tuesday 24: Franklin D Roosevelt becomes the first serving US President to visit Hawaii.

Wednesday 25: The Austrian dictator Englebert Dollfuss is assassinated.

Thursday 26: Martial law is declared in Minneapolis, Minnesota, as the general strike there worsens.

Friday 27: The worst air disaster of the year occurs when a Swissair Curtis Condor crashes near Tuttlingen, Germany. All 12 passengers and crew are killed.

Saturday 28: Albert Stevens and Orvil Anderson make a record ascent to 18,475 m (60,613 ft) above Dakota in the high-altitude balloon *Explorer*. Technical problems cause the balloon to burst into flames and plummet to the ground; the crew escape via parachutes when only 500 feet from impact.

Sunday 29: Rene Dreyfus wins the Belgian Grand Prix.

Monday 30: The western film *The Star Packer* starring John Wayne is released.

Tuesday 31: Two men found guilty of the assassination of Englebert Dollfuss on 25 July are executed.

August
1934

Germany's President Hindenburg dies on 3 August.

Wednesday 1: Pope Pius XI becomes the first Pope to travel outside Rome since 1869. Movement outside the Vatican was highly restricted by the Italian government between 1870 and 1929.

Thursday 2: Germany's President, Paul von Hindenburg dies aged 86.

Friday 3: Following the death of Germany's President Hindenburg, the roles of President and Chancellor are combined into a new role under Adolf Hitler, who becomes Fuhrer and Reich Chancellor.

Saturday 4: Mel Ott of the New York Giants becomes the first baseball player since 1899 to score six home runs in one game; he repeats the feat in 1944, becoming the only player in history to have achieved it twice.

Sunday 5: Adolf Hitler says in an interview with the *Daily Mail* that he has no desire for war, calling it 'not a romantic adventure but a ghastly catastrophe.'

Babe Ruth announces his retirement on 10 August.

Monday 6: US troops leave Haiti, which they have occupied since 1915.

Tuesday 7: The funeral of Germany's President Hindenburg takes place in Berlin, with Hitler giving the eulogy. Franz von Papen steps down as Vice-Chancellor, leaving the post vacant.

Wednesday 8: 50,000 pro-Austrian independence supporters attend a rally in Vienna, Austria, in memory of the recently assassinated leader Englebert Dollfuss.

Thursday 9: The German Evangelical Church announces its ministers must swear an oath of loyalty to Hitler.

Friday 10: The legendary baseball player Babe Ruth announces his retirement.

Saturday 11: William Beebe and Otis Barton of the USA set the world deep-sea diving record at 2,510 feet (770 m) in a bathysphere off the coast of Bermuda.

The US explorer Admiral Richard Byrd is rescued after becoming the first man to spend the winter alone in the centre of Antarctica; he had sent a radio message for help after becoming ill from a faulty gas stove.

Left: William Beebe emerges head-first from a bathysphere after a record descent on 11 August.

August 1934

Wallace Beery and Jackie Cooper in *Treasure Island*, released on 17 August.

Sunday 12: Two convicts attempt to escape by copying notorious gangster John Dillinger. Dillinger was able to bluff his way out of prison with a dummy pistol made from wood and shoe polish. Staff at prison in Baton Rouge, Louisiana, are wise to the trick however, and jail birds Bill Bryant and Raymond Candler are shot dead before they make it out.

Monday 13: The cartoon strip Li'l Abner is first published in the USA.

Tuesday 14: John S Labatt, president of Canada's Labatt brewing empire, is kidnapped near Sarnia, Ontario; criminals demand a ransom of $150,000.

'Li'l Abner' first appears in print on 13 August.

Wednesday 15: The United States occupation of Haiti formally ends.

US divers William Beebe and Otis Barton break their own record by descending to a depth of 3,028 feet (923 m) in a bathysphere off the coast of Bermuda.

Thursday 16: The Cecil B DeMille directed epic film *Cleopatra,* starring Claudette Colbert, is released.

Friday 17: Brewing magnate John S Labatt is released unharmed by kidnappers in Ontario after three days; the gang panics and flees without payment as police close in.

The film *Treasure Island* starring Wallace Beery and Jackie Cooper is released.

Saturday 18: The Japanese puppet state of Manchukuo severs diplomatic links with the USSR after a series of border disputes.

Sunday 19: Robert Turner of Muncie, Indiana, wins the USA's first All American Soap Box Derby (go-kart race) in Dayton, Ohio.

Monday 20: All German soldiers are required to swear an oath of loyalty to Adolf Hitler.

Tuesday 21: An international Jewish conference in Geneva calls for the boycotting of Germany.

The general strike in Minneapolis, Minnesota ends after three months.

Wednesday 22: The last duel is fought in Poland, between newspaper editor Ignacy Matuszewski and academic Professor Wladimir Lednizcki over a case of alleged slander.

Thursday 23: The Canadian government announces the evacuation of 40,000 families from dustbowl-stricken areas of Saskatchewan and Manitoba.

Friday 24: Dorothy Thompson becomes the first American journalist to be deported from Nazi Germany.

A young boy working on his go-kart: the first 'soap box rally is held on 19 August in Dayton, Ohio.

August 1934

Above: Claudette Colbert stars in Cleopatra, released on 16 August.

Above: Robert Donat and Elissa Landi star in *The Count of Monte Cristo*, released on 29 August.

Saturday 25: A three-hour riot takes place in the Pennsylvania State Penitentiary; forty policemen eventually quell the disturbance.

Sunday 26: Adolf Hitler addresses a crowd of 300,000 in Koblenz, Germany, calling for a return of the Saar region (occupied by France) to German control.

Monday 27: The Ira Gershwin musical *Life Begins at 08.40* opens on Broadway.

Irish fascist leader Eoin O'Duffy is banned from entering Northern Ireland.

Tuesday 28: The author Upton Sinclair is nominated as the Republican candidate for the governship of California.

Wednesday 29: The film *The Count of Monte Cristo* starring Robert Donat and Elissa Landi is released.

Thursday 30: The German government orders men under 25 to surrender their jobs to older unemployed men.

Friday 31: The painting *Nightmare of 1934* is vandalised in a New York gallery after an illegal immigrant objects to its mockery of President Roosevelt.

September 1934

Saturday 1: One million textile workers go on strike in the USA.

Sunday 2: Singer Russ Columbo dies aged 26 in a shooting accident.

Monday 3: Evangeline Booth becomes the first female leader of the Salvation Army.

Tuesday 4: The satirical novel *A Handful of Dust* by Evelyn Waugh is published.

Evangeline Booth becomes the first female leader of the Salvation Army on 3 September.

Wednesday 5: The 8th Nuremberg Rally opens in Germany.

Thursday 6: Ten men are killed and several injured during clashes between strikers and police in several US states.

Friday 7: Italian leader Benito Mussolini announces his country will support France against Germany in any future confrontation.

Saturday 8: 137 die when the American liner the SS *Morro Castle* catches fire off New Jersey.

September 1934

Above: Warner Oland stars in *Charlie Chan in London*, released on 12 September.

Above: Joseph Lyons becomes Prime Minister of Australia on 15 September.

The composer Peter Maxwell Davies is born in Salford, Lancashire (died 2016).

Sunday 9: 7000 police surround a rally in London's Hyde Park by Oswald Mosley's British Union of Fascists; trouble with left-wing groups is expected but the event concludes without incident.

Monday 10: The 8th Nuremberg Rally in Germany ends.

Tuesday 11: Cuban authorities intercept five letter bombs intended for the American Ambassador, Jefferson Caffrey.

Wednesday 12: The Baltic Entente, a treaty between Lithuania, Latvia and Estonia is signed.

The film *Charlie Chan in London* starring Warner Oland is released.

Thursday 13: The JB Priestley play *Eden End* opens in London.

Friday 14: The USSR claims Herald Island in the Chuchki Sea, following previous unsuccessful attempts by Britain and Canada.

Saturday 15: Joseph Lyons' United Australia Party wins the Australian general election, forming a coalition with the Country Party.

Sunday 16: Newspaper magnate William Randolph Hearst meets Adolf Hitler in Berlin.

A luggage label from the RMS *Queen Mary*, which is launched on 26 September.

Monday 17: The US tennis champion Maureen Connolly is born in San Diego, California (died 1969).

Tuesday 18: The League of Nations votes to admit the Soviet Union.

Wednesday 19: Brian Epstein, manager of the Beatles, is born in London (died 1967).

Thursday 20: Jim Londos defeats Ed 'Strangler' Lewis before a crowd of over 35,000 in Wrigley Field, Chicago; it is the largest professional wrestling bout in the world to this date.

Actress Sophia Loren is born in Rome.

Friday 21: Over 2700 are killed when the Muroto Typhoon hits Japan.

The singer Leonard Cohen is born in Westmount, Quebec (died 2016).

Saturday 22: The three week long textile workers' strike in the USA is called off.

266 miners are killed in a pit explosion in Gresford, Denbighshire.

Sophia Loren (shown here in 1986) is born on 20 September.

September 1934

Sunday 23: The pro-Nazi clergyman Ludwig Muller is proclaimed supreme leader of the German protestant church in Berlin Cathedral.

Monday 24: Princess Maria Pia of Bourbon-Parma and daughter of Italy's last King, Umberto II, is born in Naples, Italy.

Tuesday 25: King Victor Emmanuel III of Italy announces a pardon for all prisoners serving sentences of two years or less, in honour of the birth of his granddaughter Princess Maria.

Brigitte Bardot (shown here in 1962) is born on 28 September.

Wednesday 26: The world's largest ship to this date, the RMS *Queen Mary*, is launched by TM King George V and Queen Mary in Glasgow.

Afghanistan is admitted to the League of Nations.

Thursday 27: The first match of the new game of six-man football is played in Hebron, Nebraska.

Friday 28: 11 people are killed in a train crash at Winwick Junction near Warrington, Cheshire.

The actress Brigitte Bardot is born in Paris, France.

Saturday 29: The USA's Mutual Broadcasting System radio broadcaster goes into operation.

The play *Merrily We Roll Along* by George S Kaufman and Moss Hart premieres on Broadway.

Sunday 30: Baseball star Babe Ruth plays his final game for the New York Yankees before retirement from the full time game.

October 1934

Monday 1: The Foreign Press Association issues a warning to the German government asking them to desist from harassment of overseas reporters.

The crest of the Royal Indian Navy, inaugurated on 2 October.

The newspaper cartoon strip *Life's Like That* is first published in the USA.

Tuesday 2: The Royal Indian Navy is inaugurated following a reorganisation of the colony's coastal defence forces; the title HMIS (His Majesty's Indian Ship) is introduced.

Wednesday 3: The Cole Porter musical *Hi Diddle Diddle* opens in London; it launches the popular song Miss Otis Regrets.

Thursday 4: Alejandro Lerroux becomes Prime Minister of Spain.

Friday 5: A general strike begins in Spain.

Saturday 6: Catalonia declares itself to be an independent state, but the separatist movement under Lluis Companys is swiftly put down by government troops.

October 1934

Ginger Rogers stars in
The Gay Divorcee, **released on 12 October.**

Sunday 7: The notorious embezzler Charles Ponzi, inventor of the 'Ponzi Scheme' (pyramid scheme) is deported to his native Italy after serving 12 years in prison for fraud.

Monday 8: A general strike takes place in Cuba.

Tuesday 9: King Alexander of Yugoslavia is assassinated.

The St Louis Cardinals defeat the Detroit Tigers to win the baseball World Series.

Wednesday 10: The 32nd Roman Catholic Eucharistic Congress opens in Buenos Aires, Argentina.

Thursday 11: Bishop Hans Meiser is arrested for refusing to accept the authority of the new pro-Nazi German Evangelical Church.

Friday 12: The musical film *The Gay Divorcee* starring Fred Astaire and Ginger Rogers is released.

Saturday 13: The singer Nana Mouskouri is born in Chania, Crete.

Sunday 14: Bavarian Protestants call off church services in protest at the arrest of Bishop Meiser on 11 October.

Monday 15: The former French President and Prime Minister Raymond Poincare dies aged 74.

The MacRobertson Air Race begins on 20 October.

Left: HM King Alexander of Yugoslavia is assassinated on 9 October while on a state visit to Marseilles, France. His killer, a Macedonian nationalist, dies after being set on by an angry crowd moments later.

Tuesday 16: All German cabinet ministers swear oaths of loyalty to Adolf Hitler, and the Weimar Constitution under which he gained power is declared null and void.

Wednesday 17: Fights break out in New York City following a congressional committee hearing on whether to ban the pro-Nazi group Friends of New Germany.

Thursday 18: The funeral of recently assassinated King Alexander of Yugoslavia is held in Belgrade.

Friday 19: A joint statement from several central European countries lays the blame of King Alexander of Yugoslavia's assassination on Hungary and Italy.

Saturday 20: Twenty planes take off from RAF Mildenhall in Suffolk for the MacRobertson Air Race to Melbourne, Australia.

Nana Mouskouri (shown here in 1966) is born on 13 October.

Sunday 21: 10,000 are left homeless when a typhoon hits the Camarines Sur province of the Philippines.

Monday 22: CWA Scott and Tom Campbell Black of Great Britain win the MacRobertson Air Race, flying from England to Australia in 2 days and 22 hours in a de Havilland DH88.

October 1934

The gangster Pretty Boy Floyd dies following a shootout with police in East Liverpool, Ohio.

Tuesday 23: Francesco Agello sets the world air speed record for a piston-engined aeroplane at 440.69 mph (709.22 kmh) in a Macchi MC72 seaplane; the record has never been broken.

Jeanette Piccard becomes the first woman to enter the stratosphere, in a high altitude balloon piloted by her husband Jean.

Wednesday 24: Harry Reser and his band make the first recording of the song *Santa Claus is Coming to Town.*

Thursday 25: The new sport of midget car racing claims its first victim as driver Chet Mortemore, 24, is killed during a race in Los Angeles.

The Union Pacific railway's new streamlined service sets a speed record travelling between Los Angeles and Chicago in 38 hours 49 minutes.

Friday 26: The pianist and composer Jacques Loussier is born in Angers, France (died 2019).

Saturday 27: King Prajadhipok of Siam (Thailand) announces his abdication.

Sunday 28: The first of only four NFL American football games in which no penalties are called takes place when the Brooklyn Dodgers defeat the Pittsburgh Pirates 21-3 at Ebbet's Field, Brooklyn.

Monday 29: The Berne Trial opens in Switzerland as Jewish groups sue the Swiss fascist party for distributing anti-semitic literature.

Tuesday 30: Frank B Elser's play *The Farmer Wants A Wife* opens on Broadway.

Wednesday 31: The Chicago World's Fair closes.

November 1934

Thursday 1: British politician Winston Churchill warns that Germany is rearming 'secretly, illegally and rapidly.'

Friday 2: An all star American baseball team led by Babe Ruth and Lou Gehrig begins a tour of Japan.

Saturday 3: Charles Kingsford Smith completes the first eastward air crossing of the Pacific, flying from Brisbane to San Francisco in the *Lady Southern Cross*.

Sunday 4: Madras play Mysore at cricket in the first match of India's Ranji Trophy.

Charles Kingsford Smith, shown here with his wife Mary, makes aviation history on 3 November.

November 1934

Monday 5: German churches are ordered to include prayers for the welfare of Adolf Hitler in all Sunday services.

Tuesday 6: In the US mid-term elections the encumbent Democratic Party increases its seats; the vote is seen as an endorsement of Roosevelt's 'New Deal' economic reforms.

Jean Harlow announces her divorce on 10 November.

Wednesday 7: The French and German governments announce a plebiscite will be held in January 1935 on ownership of the Saar region between the two countries, occupied by France since the end of the Great War.

Godfrey Huggins becomes Prime Minister of Southern Rhodesia.

Thursday 8: Pierre-Étienne Flandin becomes Prime Minister of France.

Friday 9: The astronomer Carl Sagan is born in New York City (died 1996).

Gabriel Reyes becomes the first native Archbishop of the Phillippines.

The Shrine of Remembrance in Melbourne, Australia, is opened on 11 November.

A 1934 Chevrolet Master Sedan. The ten millionth Chevrolet is produced on 13 November.

Saturday 10: The Hollywood star Jean Harlow announces her divorce from cinematographer Harold Rosson.

Sunday 11: The Shrine of Remembrance war memorial in Melbourne, Australia, is opened.

Monday 12: The cult leader Charles Manson is born in Cincinnati, Ohio (died 2017).

Tuesday 13: The ten millionth Chevrolet car is produced.

All Italian teachers are ordered to wear the uniform of the fascist party in school hours.

Wednesday 14: England defeats Italy 3-2 in a violent football match which becomes known as the Battle of Highbury.

Thursday 15: Large sections of the ancient city of Carthage are discovered by archaeologists in Tunisia.

Friday 16: Bob Olin becomes World Lightweight boxing champion when he defeats Maxie Rosenbloom at Madison Square Garden, New York.

Alice Liddell, Lewis Carrol's inspiration for the character of Alice in Alice in Wonderland, dies aged 82.

Saturday 17: Paraguay makes major advances in the Chaco War against

Pierre-Étienne Flandin becomes French PM on 8 November.

November 1934

Brig-Gen Smedley Butler is accused of plotting a coup in the USA on 20 November.

Bolivia, capturing seven forts on the main defensive line.

Sunday 18: The Japanese government indicates it is preparing to withdraw from the Washington Naval Treaty of 1922 which limits its navy; it pulls out of the agreement in 1936.

Monday 19: The *New York Daily News* runs an expose of match-fixing in professional wrestling, leading to plummeting attendances at matches.

Tuesday 20: Plans to overthrow the US government in a military coup led by a former army officer, Smedley Butler, are revealed. Despite a year long enquiry into the plot, no charges are ever brought against the alleged organisers.

Wednesday 21: The musical *Anything Goes* by Cole Porter opens on Broadway.

Thursday 22: The philosopher Bertrand Russell is divorced from his wife Dora.

Friday 23: Darius Milhaud's Piano Concert Number One is first performed, in Paris.

The Flying Scotsman sets a rail speed record on 30 November.

The film *Anne of Green Gables* starring Dawn O'Day is released.

Saturday 24: The ANZAC war memorial in Sydney, Australia, is unveiled.

Missionaries throughout southern China are forced to evacuate as communist forces flee south in the wake of the advance of nationalist leader Chiang Kai Shek.

Sunday 25: The French government announces an alliance and defence pact with Soviet Russia.

Laurel and Hardy star in *Babes in Toyland*, released on 30 November.

Monday 26: Turkey's President Mustafa Kemal adopts the surname Ataturk ('father of the Turks') as noble titles are outlawed.

Tuesday 27: The notorious gangster George 'Baby Face' Nelson is killed in a shoot-out with FBI agents in Barrington, Illinois.

Wednesday 28: Spectators pack a London court in the hope of hearing lurid details in the divorce case between Lord Ashley and his wife Sylvia, in which the Hollywood star Douglas Fairbanks is cited as co-respondent. The proceedings, however, last only ten minutes.

Thursday 29: Prince George, Duke of Kent, is married to Princess Marina of Greece and Denmark at Westminster Abbey.

Friday 30: Lázaro Cárdenas becomes President of Mexico.

The Flying Scotsman becomes the first steam locomotive to exceed 100mph.

The comedy film *Babes in Toyland* starring Laurel and Hardy is released.

December 1934

Saturday 1: Following the assassination of Sergey Kirov, mayor of Leningrad, Soviet leader Josef Stalin begins the Great Purge of the country's communist party.

Sunday 2: The first performance is given by the jazz group Hot Club de France, led by Django Reinhardt and Stephane Grappelli, in Paris.

Tuesday 3: The Italian African colonies of Cyrenaica, Tripolitania and Fezzan are merged to become Italian Libya.

Wednesday 4: Wilhelm Furtwängler, director of the Berlin Philharmonic and State Opera, resigns in protest over Nazi party controls on the arts.

Thursday 5: Women in Turkey are granted the vote.

Left: one of the first air mail letters sent from England to Australia when the service begins on 8 December.

December 1934

Dame Judi Dench is born on 9 December.

Friday 6: Charles Michael, Duke of Mecklenburg, dies aged 71.

Saturday 7: A trans-Pacific telephone line between the USA and Japan is inaugurated.

Sunday 8: Air mail services between Britain and Australia begin.

Monday 9: The actress Dame Judi Dench is born in Heworth, Yorkshire.

Tuesday 10: Britain's Arthur Henderson MP receives the Nobel Peace Prize for his work with the Geneva Disarmament Conference.

Wednesday 11: US citizen Elizabeth Steele is released from prison in Germany after being held for four months on suspicion of espionage. She later plays herself in the 1936 film, *I Was A Captive In Nazi Germany.*

Thursday 12: The British government announces its withdrawal from the naval disarmament talks between Britain, the USA and Japan due to a lack of progress.

Friday 13: New York City's Mark Hellinger Theater opens.

Saturday 14: 15 people are killed when Adolf Hitler's official train hits a bus on a level crossing.

Sunday 15: The US government approves an unemployment insurance scheme.

Monday 16: The Fascist International Conference opens in Montreux, Switzerland.

Django Reinhardt first plays with the Hot Club de France on 2 December.

December 1934

Tuesday 17: 1000 people are made homeless in Rome as the Tiber bursts its banks.

Wednesday 18: Italy's Province of Latina is founded.

Thursday 19: The government of Japan renounces the Washington Naval Treaty after Britain and the USA refuse to allow them parity of re-armament.

Leslie Howard and Merle Oberon star in *The Scarlet Pimpernel*, released on 23 December.

Friday 20: Germany bans the abuse of any Nazi Party uniforms or insignia.

Saturday 21: Sergei Prokofiev's Opus 60, *Lieutenant Kijé*, is first performed.

Sunday 22: British, Italian, Dutch and Swedish troops enter the Saarland territory between France and Germany to oversee the plebiscite to be held in January.

Monday 23: The adventure film *The Scarlet Pimpernel* starring Leslie Howard is released.

Tuesday 24: Leading Nazi Party member Rudolf Hess gives a Christmas message to the German people, stating that Adolf Hitler is 'the Chancellor of Peace.'

Wednesday 25: 15 people are killed in a train crash in Dundas, Ontario, Canada.

The comedy play *Accent on Youth* opens on Broadway.

Thursday 26: The Montevideo Convention, opposing US intervention in Latin America, goes into effect.

Helen Richey becomes the first female commercial pilot on 31 December.

Friday 27: The Shah of Persia announces that from 21 March 1935 the country will be renamed Iran.

Saturday 28: The comedy drama film *Bright Eyes* starring Shirley Temple is released.

Actress Dame Maggie Smith is born in Ilford, Essex.

Sunday 29: The musician George Gershwin performs at the White House for President Roosevelt.

Monday 30: 5 people are killed in an attack by communist agitators on church-goers in Mexico City.

Tuesday 31: The USA's Helen Richey becomes the world's first commercial woman pilot.

Dutch troops are inspected before departing for peacekeeping duties in the Saarland, 22 December.

More titles from Montpelier Publishing

A Little Book of Limericks:
Funny Rhymes for all the Family
ISBN 9781511524124

Scottish Jokes: A Wee Book of
Clean Caledonian Chuckles
ISBN 9781495297366

The Old Fashioned Joke Book:
Gags and Funny Stories
ISBN 9781514261989

Non-Religious Funeral Readings:
Philosophy and Poetry for Secular
Services
ISBN 9781500512835

Large Print Jokes: Hundreds of
Gags in Easy-to-Read Type
ISBN 9781517775780

**Spiritual Readings for Funerals
and Memorial Services**
ISBN 9781503379329

Victorian Murder: True Crimes,
Confessions and Executions
ISBN 9781530296194

Large Print Prayers: A Prayer for
Each Day of the Month
ISBN 9781523251476

**A Little Book of Ripping Riddles
and Confounding Conundrums**
ISBN 9781505548136

Vinegar uses: over 150 ways to use
vinegar
ISBN 9781512136623

Large Print Wordsearch:
100 Puzzles in Easy-to-Read Type
ISBN 9781517638894

The Pipe Smoker's Companion
ISBN 9781500441401

The Book of Church Jokes
ISBN 9781507620632

Bar Mitzvah Notebook
ISBN 9781976007781

Jewish Jokes
ISBN 9781514845769

Large Print Address Book
ISBN 9781539820031

How to Cook Without a Kitchen:
Easy, Healthy and Low-Cost Meals
9781515340188

Large Print Birthday Book
ISBN 9781544670720

Retirement Jokes
ISBN 9781519206350

Take my Wife: Hilarious Jokes of
Love and Marriage
ISBN 9781511790956

Welsh Jokes: A Little Book of
Wonderful Welsh Wit
ISBN 9781511612241

1001 Ways to Save Money: Thrifty
Tips for the Fabulously Frugal!
ISBN 9781505432534

Order online from Amazon or from your local bookshop

Printed in Great Britain
by Amazon

37431372R00036